www.25Careers.com

Ordering Information: Special discounts are available on quantity purchases by bookstores, wholesalers, corporations, associations, and others. For details please visit us on the web at:
www.25Careers.com

25 CAREERS YOU NEVER KNEW EXISTED

COLORING & ACTIVITY BOOK

By:
Tracy Balan

Illustration By:
Shiela Marie Alejandro

"Career Day"

Welcome to career day!
My name is Tracy, today I will be introducing you to my 25 friends
and their careers you never knew existed.

Let's get started!

Find the Careers

In the chart below, circle all the careers you will be learning today. Don't forget to look forward, backward, up, down and diagonally.

```
E  E  G  L  P  A  A  N  E  C  I  O  V  V  W  A  P  P  D  I
C  L  C  D  D  S  V  N  O  D  R  Y  T  I  R  B  E  L  E  C
I  I  R  E  T  N  I  A  P  I  Y  E  L  E  M  A  G  R  S  M
F  B  I  M  C  I  F  F  A  R  T  O  L  I  Z  R  J  T  I  O
D  O  W  Y  L  L  O  H  W  E  A  A  T  L  E  Z  R  G  G  R
J  M  D  F  H  C  E  E  P  S  N  H  C  N  O  E  K  S  N  E
W  O  P  R  E  P  O  R  T  E  R  G  G  O  N  R  B  E  E  P
S  T  U  N  T  P  E  R  S  O  N  I  I  D  L  R  T  T  R  M
O  U  W  I  P  I  O  M  D  B  S  F  O  N  I  P  U  N  T  U
Z  A  W  E  N  N  I  J  A  E  C  L  O  D  E  S  K  S  O  J
S  V  T  B  O  S  T  L  D  T  O  S  G  O  N  E  I  C  M  C
T  V  G  M  R  J  T  I  A  G  R  E  F  P  D  L  R  R  E  A
C  R  E  A  T  O  R  R  I  N  P  E  E  W  Y  E  W  E  C  T
B  R  R  Y  L  Q  L  S  U  K  O  E  S  T  A  V  R  P  H  C
T  E  S  T  E  R  T  L  G  C  L  S  S  S  A  A  I  P  A  H
B  N  E  P  L  L  U  B  E  S  T  R  R  H  S  T  T  O  N  E
C  R  O  S  S  W  O  R  D  R  I  O  A  E  A  O  E  H  I  R
H  D  E  S  I  G  N  E  R  A  M  H  R  I  P  R  R  S  C  S
N  M  O  B  I  L  E  S  H  O  S  G  R  E  E  N  S  M  A  N
Y  R  A  N  I  L  U  C  R  E  T  S  A  O  C  M  P  K  O  N
```

AIR TRAFFIC CONTROLLER	CULINARY TRENDOLOGIST	PERSONAL SHOPPER
ASTRONOMER	ELEVATOR MECHANIC	ROLLER COASTER ENGINEER
AUTOMOBILE DESIGNER	FOOD STYLIST	SET DESIGNER
BRIDGE PAINTER	GREENSMAN	SLEEP INSTRUCTOR
BULLPEN CATCHER	HOLLYWOD STUNTPERSON	SPEECH WRITER
CELEBRITY HAIRSTYLIST	ICE CREAM TASTER	TOY CREATOR
COURT REPORTER	LOCATION SCOUT	VIDEO GAME TESTER
CROSSWORD PUZZLE WRITER	MATRESS JUMPER	VOICE OVER ARTIST
	MOBILE APP DESIGNER	

This is my friend Bill. He is an Air Traffic Controller.
Air Traffic Controllers are people trained to keep
airplanes safe and orderly in the sky.
He helps planes from crashing into each other by keeping a
safe distance between them.

Let's look up into the sky with Angela. She is an Astronomer.

An astronomer is someone who studies the universe and everything in it.
This includes the stars, planets and galaxies.

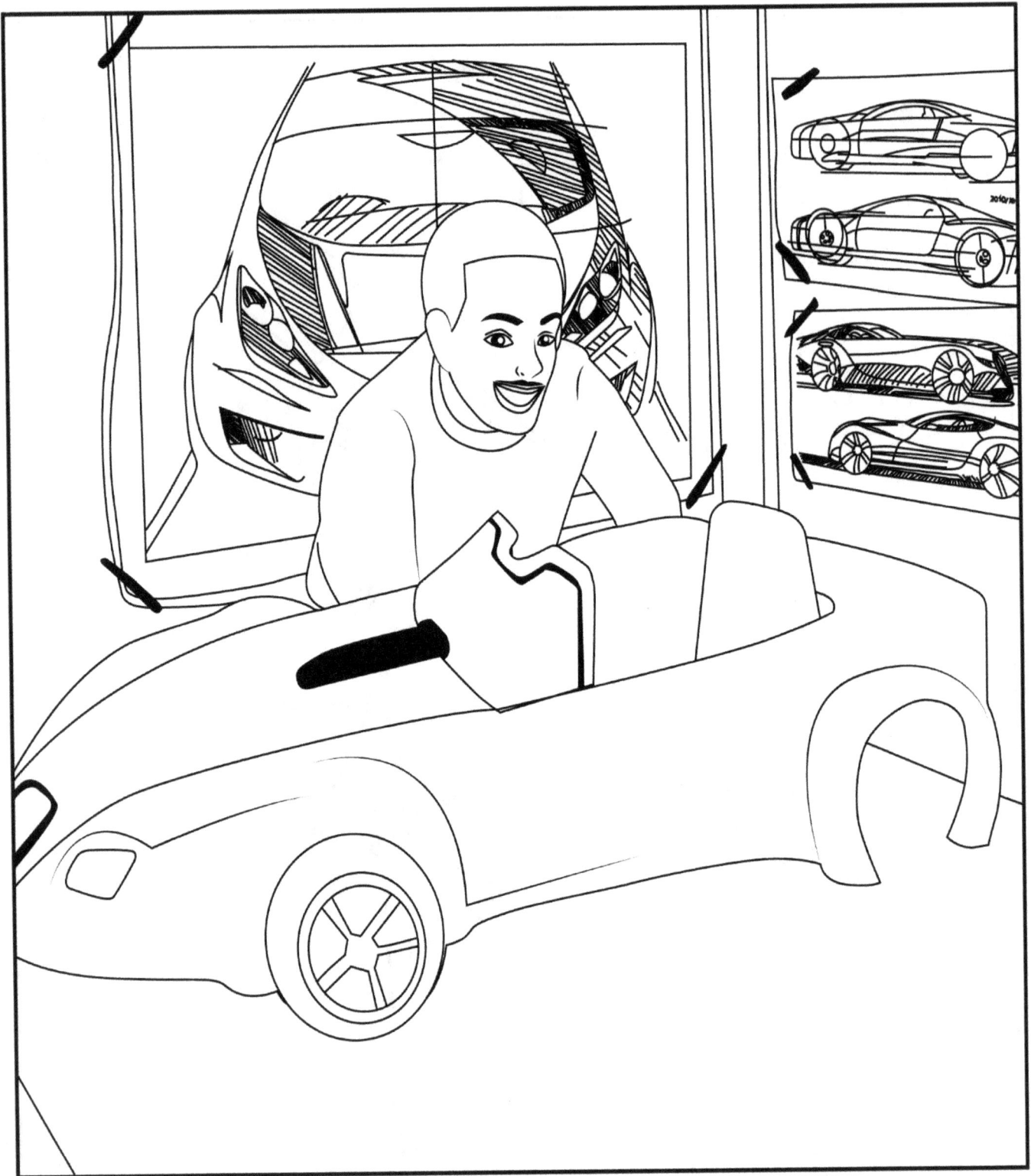

This is my friend Joseph. He is an Automobile Designer.

An automobile designer is a person designing the appearance and function of automobiles, including cars, trucks, vans, buses, and even motorcycles. The interior and exterior of every vehicle is designed by automobile designers.

Connect the dots

Connect the dots to reveal Joseph's new car design.

Look up there! That's my friend Sara! She is a Bridge Painter.

A bridge painter is in charge of painting bridges every three to seven years with a special paint to help the bridge from rusting.

I love coming to Baseball games because I get to see my friend Clayton! He is a Bullpen Catcher.

A Bullpen Catcher is someone who catches the fly or foul balls and throws it back to the pitcher.

If you are ever at the Court house, stop and see my friend Ashley. No, she is not a Lawyer or a Judge. She is the Court Reporter.

A Court Reporter is a person who takes spoken or recorded speech and puts it into written form, using special equipment to produce official transcripts for official court proceedings.

Find What Does Not Belong

Look at the picture closely and find the 7 things that do not belong in a court room.

This is my friend Kevin. He is a Crossword Puzzle Writer.

A Crossword Puzzle Writer's job is to build and create crossword puzzles for newspapers, magazines and technology games.

Have you ever wondered why your favorite restaurant added a new burger to its menu? Well it's because of my friend, Sandra! She is a Culinary Trendologist (Trend-o-log-ist).

A culinary trendologist (trend-o-log-ist) keeps an eye on food news, blogs, social media and published recipes to determine which foods will be the favorite for days, weeks and months from now.

This is my friend Harry! He is an
Elevator Mechanic.

An elevator mechanic is someone who constructs, repairs and
service elevators and even escalators sometimes.

Missing Elevator Buttons

Help Harry fix the elevator by filling in the missing numbers on the elevator buttons.

(1)	(9)	(17)
(2)	(10)	(18)
( )	(11)	( )
(4)	(12)	(20)
( )	( )	( )
( )	(14)	(22)
(7)	( )	(23)
(8)	(16)	( )

(stop)   (help)

Say hello to my friend, Cynthia! She's around food all day as a Food Stylist.

A food stylist is someone who prepares and styles food for advertisement and magazine photoshoots.

Do you love plants? Well, not as much as my friend Ethan. He is a Greensman.

A greensman is in charge of designing and arranging all of the plant materials, both real and fake, on a film set and in TV commercials.

Matching Flowers

Here are four sets of flowers. Match and then color the identical flowers.

A.

C.

H.

B.

D.

G.

E.

F.

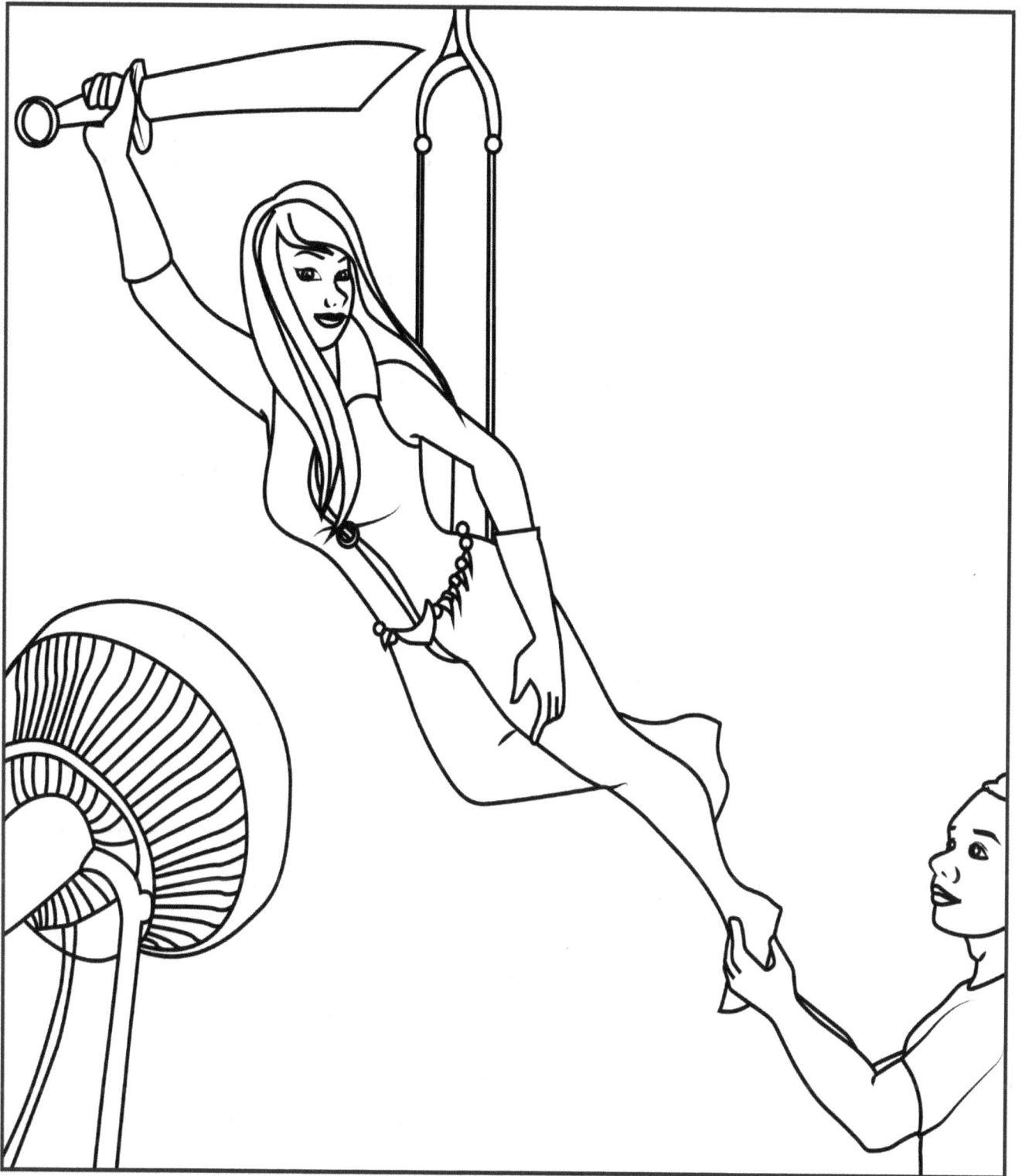

This is my friend Carline. She is a Hollywood Stunt Person.

A Hollywood stunt person pretends to be a famous actor or actress taking punches, blowing up explosions and taking all the risk.

My friend Jake has the coolest job. He is an Ice Cream Taster.

An ice cream taster has a degree in either Food Sciences or Nutrition. They evaluate ice cream for taste, texture, and smell.

This is my friend Rochelle. All she does is travel around the world as a Location Scout.
A location scout finds proper locales and backdrops for every scene in a film, TV show or other work that is filmed or photographed.

Maze

Help Rochelle find a great beach location for a new movie!

Do you know how to jump up and down? Let's help my friend
Christopher. He is a Mattress Jumper.
A mattress jumper makes sure that your mattress is bed-ready
for you to sleep. This involves them compressing the layers by
jumping across the mattress surface.

This is my friend Maxi. She is a
Mobile App Designer.
An application designer is a person who designs software for
cell phones, tablets and all types of mobile devices. I'm sure
you have used one of her applications before.

My friend David loves to shop, so he is a Personal Shopper.

A personal shopper is an individual who is paid to help another to purchase goods, either by accompanying them while shopping or by shopping on their behalf.

What Comes Next

Look at the pattern and circle what comes next from the clothing that David has laid out!

This is my friend Carole. She spends a lot of time at amusement parks, and she's a Rollercoaster Engineer.

A Rollercoaster Engineer is the designer behind a roller coaster's loops, drops, and turns. There challenge is to build bigger and faster rollercoasters.

Shhhhhhh....... Quiet on set! My friend Aston is a Set Designer.

A set designer creates and designs the sets used in performance art, movies, TV scenery and plays. At times, designing these sets may be as simple as arranging a few pieces of furniture on a stage. Other times, it may be as complicated as recreating a complex location, such as the inside of a spaceship.

How many words?

Think hard and see how many words you can make from the word

SET DESIGNER

_____   _____   _____

_____   _____   _____

_____   _____   _____

_____   _____   _____

_____   _____   _____

Can't Sleep? Then you need my friend Regine. She is a
Sleep Instructor.
A sleep instructor helps the overworked catch their zzzzz's with
mind and body exercises, but their advice doesn't only apply at
night. They also help clients boost productivity, alertness, and
performance at work to reduce nighttime stress.

This is my friend Antonio. He has a very important job as a Speech Writer.

A speech writer is someone who writes speeches for either the president or senior public officials. They even help people write speeches for presentations, graduations and even weddings to name a few.

Yes we are in a Toy Factory! Because my friend Judy is a
Toy Creator.

A toy creator designs and helps improve new and old toys. These toys include board games, educational games and collectibles.

Color by Numbers

Judy created a new teddy bear, color it in by matching the numbers to the color on the bear.

1. Red   2. Brown   3. Pink   4. Yellow

This is my friend David. He is a Video Game Tester.

A video game tester is someone who plays video games all day. They help developers find errors in games to help improve the system.

This is my friend Katie. She is a Voice-Over Artist.

A voice-over artist is a person who lends their voice to be used in commercials, movies, cartoon characters and that's just to name a few.

Last but not least! I am a Celebrity Hairstylist.

A celebrity hairstylist is someone who does celebrity hair. They travel the world for celebrity clients to do their hair for performances, award shows, movies and TV shows!

How Many?

Help Tracy unpack! How many tools does she have in her bag?

Comb	Brush	Blow Dryer	Hairspray	Curling Iron
___	___	___	___	___

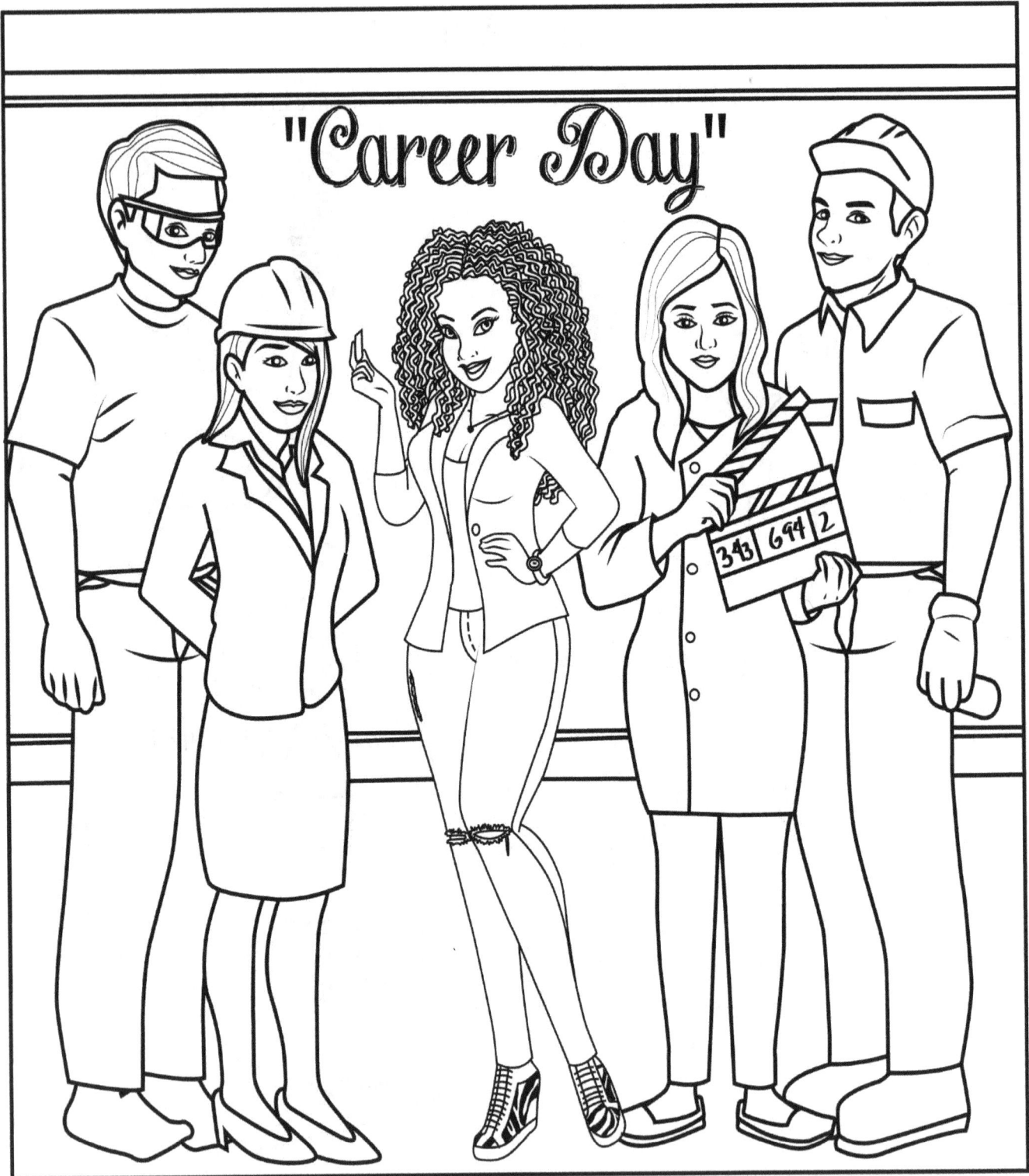

"Career Day"

These are all my friends!

Hope you enjoyed Career Day!

Answers

Find The Careers

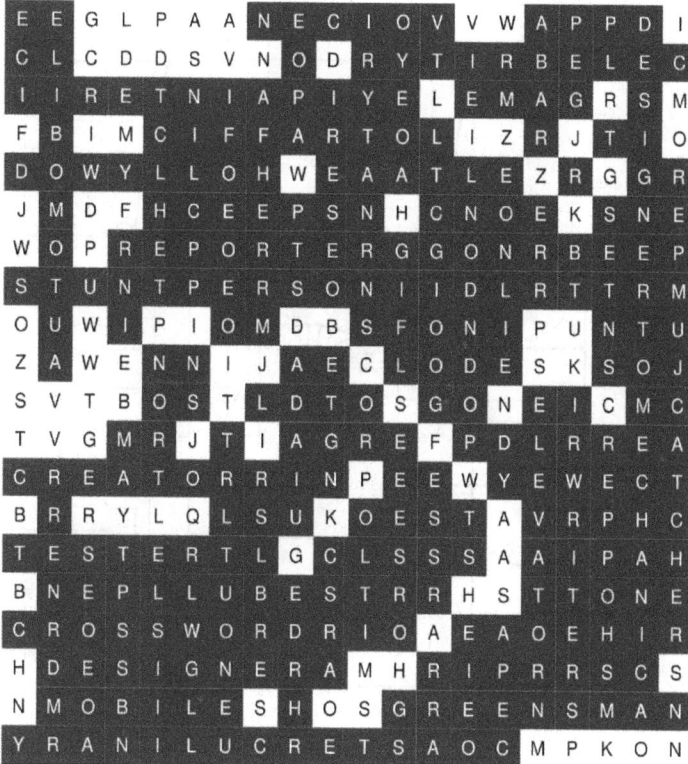

Connect The Dots

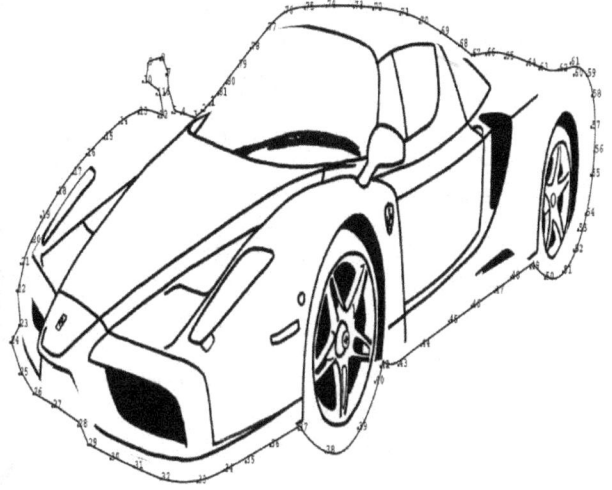

Find What Does Not Belong

Missing Elevator Buttons

Answers

Matching Flowers

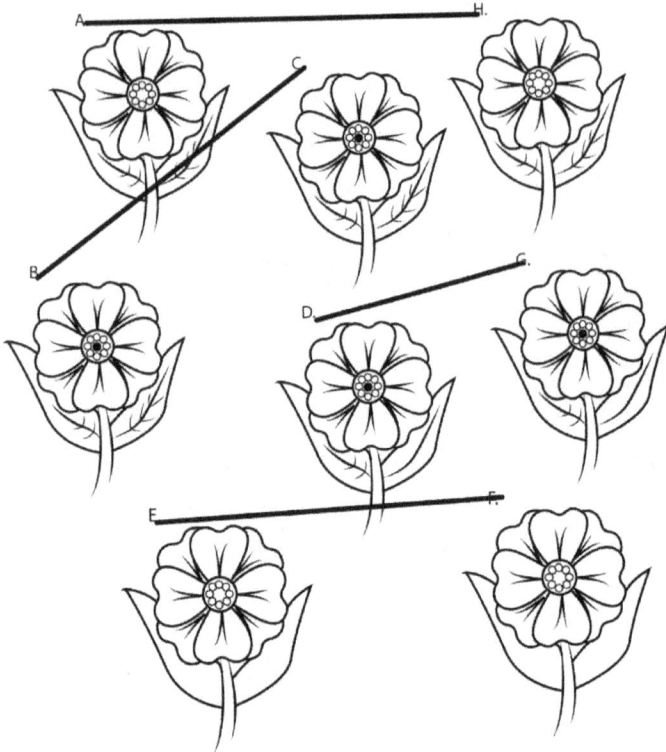

Maze

What Comes Next

How Many Words

SET DESIGNER

set	designer	dress
sign	green	sin
rest	gin	deer
nest	sent	rinse
ten	send	ride

Answers

Color By Numbers

1. Red   2. Brown   3. Pink   4. Yellow

How Many

Comb	Brush	Blow Dryer	Hairspray	Curling Iron
5	5	6	5	6

Thank you

First and foremost I thank **GOD** for putting this book in me. Thank you for giving me the ambition to execute and bring this book to life.

To my family and friends, thank you for your continued support as I have traveled down the road of my life and career evaluation.

And last but not least to my better half. I want to think you for supporting me as I have gone though all my career paths. Thank you for your continued love and belief in me with all my dreams day in and day out.

Dedication

This book is dedicated to my oldest sister Sandra Balan who has passed but I know is always watching over me.

ABOUT THE AUTHOR

Celebrity hairstylist Tracy Balan is a Jack of all trades and the master of every one! This gifted hairstylist, motivational speaker, author and television host has a resume that makes even the most talented professional quake in their shoes. Though her path to entrepreneurial excellence has been unconventional, every opportunity Tracy embraced propelled her further up the career ladder to phenomenal success!

From business school, to a three year stint with the United States Military Intelligence Department to the prestigious Empire Beauty School, this Brooklyn, New York native never lost sight of her dream to create unique styling techniques that would revolutionize beauty salons everywhere! Ms. Balan has become one of the world's leading masters of extensions. Her signature brand of elegance and beauty has thrust her onto the world stage with a vengeance! No one who meets Tracy Balan will ever forget her or her inspired creations.

As a motivational speaker, Tracy shares her story—the joys, the pain, the struggles and the incredible success and favor now lavished upon her. Her goal? To empower women around the world to pursue their dreams by teaching them how to be true to themselves. As the host of the Lifetime's "Girlfriend Intervention", Ms. Balan has given notice to the world that women will not play small. They will play big, take center stage in their lives and go home with the prize! In her own words: "Find what's beautiful for you, not others."

To learn more about the unstoppable Ms. Tracy Balan, visit www.TracyBalan.com and indulge yourself in a swath of luxurious pleasure that will forever transform your life!